CW00621645

Name-Changing:
A Practical Guide

Fourmat Publishing

By the same author:

Adoption Practice and Procedure   (Fourmat Publishing, 1984)
Wardship: The Law and Practice   (Fourmat Publishing, 1986)
Custodianship: The Law and Practice   (Fourmat Publishing, 1986)
A Guide to Inheritance Claims   (Fourmat Publishing, 1989)

The author is also a contributor to Butterworth's *Wills, Probate and Administration Service*

Name-Changing:
A Practical Guide

by Nasreen Pearce, Barrister
A Registrar of the Principal
Registry of the Family Division

London
Fourmat Publishing
1990

ISBN 1 85190 089 6

First published 1990

© Fourmat Publishing
133 Upper Street Islington London N1 1QP

Typeset by Pentacor Ltd, High Wycombe, Bucks
Printed in Great Britain by Billing & Sons Ltd, Worcester

Preface

The aim of this short handbook is to provide a simple, practical and straightforward guide to the law and procedure relating to changing a person's name. A concise statement of the law is provided, and, in respect of a change in a child's name, the application of the general principles is illustrated by case law. Where possible, the provisions of the Children Act 1989 (which is not yet in force) have been referred to.

The book is not intended to be a definitive text and, for example, does not deal with the specialised law relating to bodies corporate or to ships. Although some instances of the requirements of professional bodies have been included, the ground covered is not exhaustive. In all such cases, reference should be made to the appropriate professional organisation for their specific requirements.

Finally, I would like to thank the registrars of the various professional bodies referred to in Chapter 6 for putting me on the right track regarding their present rules and requirements.

Nasreen Pearce
January 1990

Contents

Table of cases

Chapter 1

Introduction

It is often asked, what is in name? To some it means very little. To others it means such a great deal that they would like their names changed. A change of name could assist in disassociating them from a past they wish to leave behind or from a relationship which would be better forgotten. A change of name could be a way of confirming a change in status or resolving an embarrassment. It may be that a person simply does not like the name given to him or her. Whatever the reason, the matter is of sufficient significance that they would like their name changed. It is often believed that it might prove impossible to make the change, or that it might be too difficult or involve a great deal of expense and complicated legal process.

In reality, depending on the circumstances of each individual case, the change may be effected quite simply and at no cost or at very little expense. The law does not prescribe any limitations on the person's right to change his or her name. A name is a means of identification and the law is merely concerned with the question of whether the assumed name is the one by which the person has come to be known and identified. Provided, therefore, that in adopting a new name the person does not thereby intend to deceive or defraud another, a person may change his or her name as he or she pleases. He may change his forename and or his surname. He may add names to his original name or surname, or substitute it with others, or simply re-arrange the names.

A person acquires his original name when his name is registered at birth under the Births and Deaths Registration

Act 1953. Provision is made under that Act, and under the Family Law Reform Act 1987, for re-registration in certain circumstances (see further pages 5 to 17).

A person may have had his forename conferred on him at baptism. There is some uncertainty as to whether a Christian name can be changed or not, and if so, how. In *R* v *Smith* (1865), it was observed that a Christian name may not be changed. In *Re Parrott* (1946), Vaisey J said that there may be only three ways in which a Christian name may be changed; see further page 46. A Christian name may, however, be changed on confirmation.

On marriage, there is no legal requirement for a woman to change her maiden name but women usually choose to take their husband's surname.

An adult may change his name simply by becoming known by the assumed name by reputation, by advertising the fact that he has relinquished his former name and confirming the name by which he desires to be known. A statutory declaration to that effect may also be made.

In order to avoid confusion and doubt, the most common formal method of changing a name is by deed poll. Other more complicated and expensive methods include a change by an Act of Parliament and royal licence.

Those who follow a profession may change their names like any other individual, but the governing body or organisation of the profession of which the person is a member may require compliance with the requirements of their rules and regulations, or may require formal evidence of a change of name before recognising the change or altering the register, if a register is kept.

Changing the name of a person who is under the age of eighteen years can be simple if the parents agree. If, however, they do not, legal process may be necessary as there are restrictions on effecting a change of name of a child; see further Chapter 3.

Where a child is to be adopted and the proposed adopters wish the child to be known by a different name, the name may be changed provided the prescribed procedure is followed; see page 48.

An alien too may change his name, but there are certain

restrictions which apply. These are discussed further at page 31.

Thus, save in respect of doubts regarding the change of a name given on baptism, and the restrictions imposed on the change of the name of a child, and in relation to those who are regarded as aliens, there appears to be no legal objection or bar to a person's changing his or her name.

Chapter 2

Change under the Births and Deaths Registration Act

1. Registration of birth

The Births and Deaths Registration Act 1953 s 1 requires the birth of every child born in England and Wales to be registered by the Registrar of Births and Deaths for the sub-district in which the child was born, by entering in a register kept for that sub-district such particulars concerning the birth as may be prescribed.

Where a new-born child is found exposed and no information as to the place of birth is available, the birth must be registered by the Registrar for the sub-district where the child is found.

Section 2 of the 1953 Act makes it a duty:

(a) of the father and the mother of the child; and

(b) in the case of the death or the inability of the father and mother, of each other qualified informant,

to give to the Registrar, within forty-two days of the birth of the child, the information of the particulars required to be registered concerning the birth of a child; and, in the presence of the Registrar, to sign the register.

In the case of a new-born child who is found exposed, the duty of giving the information and of signing the register is placed on the person who found the child, and on any person in whose charge the child may be placed.

Rule 7 of the Registration of Births and Deaths Regulations

1987 (SI 1987 No 2088) provides that the particulars concerning a live-birth required to be registered are those set out in Form 1 (see page 61).

2. Re-registration or alteration of name within twelve months

A child's name may be altered within twelve months of registration of its birth, but in this case the name must be re-registered. Section 13 of the Births and Deaths Registration Act 1953 provides that where, before the expiration of twelve months from the date of the registration of the birth of any child, the name by which it was registered is altered, or, if it was registered without a name, and a name is later given to the child, the Registrar or Superintendent Registrar having the custody of the register in which the birth was registered is to make an entry in the register upon delivery to him of a certificate in the prescribed form.

Rule 14(1) of the Registration of Births and Deaths Regulations 1987 prescribes two forms of certificate, namely:

(a) where the name was altered or given in baptism, the certficate must be in Form 3; see page 63;

(b) where the name was altered or given otherwise than in baptism, it must be in Form 4; see page 63.

If the name was altered or given in baptism, the certificate in Form 3 must be signed either by the officiating minister or by the person having custody of the baptismal register. If the name was not given to the child in baptism, Form 4 is the appropriate form of certificate and it must be signed by the "father, mother or guardian of the child or other person procuring the name of the child to be altered or given" (s 13(1)(b), Births and Deaths Registration Act 1953).

Upon delivery to him of the appropriate certificate, the Registrar must enter the new name or altered name, without any erasure, in the register: s 13(1). The Registrar or Superintendent Registrar having custody of the register in which the birth is entered must, in pursuance of s 13(1), enter in space 17 of the entry the name shown in the certificate, followed by the surname recorded in space 2 of the entry and:

(a) if the entry is made on production of a certificate that the name was given in baptism he will insert the words "by baptism" and insert the date on which the child was baptised;

(b) if the entry is made on production of a certificate that the name was given other than on baptism, he will add the words "on certificate of naming dated the ......", and insert the date on which the certificate was signed.

Note that the time limit within which the above procedure may be adopted is twelve months from the date of registration of birth. It is not possible to use the above procedure for re-registration where the name is given or altered after the expiration of twelve months from the date on which the birth was first registered. The only alternative would be to make a statutory declaration to the effect that the birth certificate and the baptismal certificate where the child has been baptised relate to the same child.

3. Change to correct error in registration

Section 29(1) of the Births and Deaths Registration Act 1953 provides that no alteration shall be made in any register of live-births, still-births or deaths except as authorised by that Act or by any other Act.

Section 29(2) makes provision for clerical errors to be corrected, by any person authorised in that behalf by the Registrar General, in the prescribed manner and subject to the prescribed conditions.

An error of fact or substance in a register may be corrected by entry in the margin (without any alteration of the original entry) by the officer having custody of the register, upon production to him of a statutory declaration. The statutory declaration must set out the nature of the error and the true facts of the case. It must be made and delivered to the officer by two qualified informants of the birth with reference to which the error has been made, or in default of two qualified informants, then by two credible persons having knowledge of the true facts of the case.

The Act does not require the registration of the birth of a

child to be made by *both* parents. Either parent may register the birth, so that in the case of a mother of a child who left her husband before the birth of the child, and then changed her surname and on the birth of the child registered the child in her assumed surname, it was held that she did not make an error of fact which could be corrected under the provisions of s 29(3) of the Act: see *D* v *B (Surname: Birth Registration)* (1979).

4. Registration of birth where parents are not married

Section 10 of the Births and Deaths Registration Act 1953, as substituted by s 24 of the Family Law Reform Act 1987, sets out the procedure to be followed and the evidence required before the name of any person may be registered as father when a birth is first registered, where the parents are not married to each other at the time the child was born.

In these circumstances, the Registrar will not enter the name of any person as father of the child except:

(a) at the joint request of the mother and the person stating himself to be the father of the child (in which case that person must sign the register together with the mother); or

(b) at the request of the mother on production of—

    (i) a declaration in the prescribed form (Form 2; see page 62) made by the mother stating that that person is the father of the child; and

    (ii) a statutory declaration made by that person stating himself to be the father of the child; or

(c) at the request of that person on production of—

    (i) a declaration in the prescribed form by that person stating himself to be the father of the child; and

    (ii) a statutory declaration made by the mother stating that that person is the father of the child; or

(d) at the request of the mother or that person (which

shall in either case be made in writing) on production of—

  (i) a certified copy of a relevant order; and

  (ii) if the child has attained the age of sixteen, the written consent of the child to the registration of the person as his father.

A relevant order under (d)(i) above means any of the following orders:

(a) an order under s 4 of the Family Law Reform Act 1987 giving the natural father of the child full parental rights and duties with respect to the child;

(b) an order under s 9 of the Guardianship of Minors Act 1971 which gives the natural father any parental right with respect to the child; and

(c) an order under s 11B of the Guardianship of Minors Act 1971 (as substituted by s 12 of the Family Law Reform Act 1987) which requires that person to make any financial provision for the child.

See also pages 28 to 29 for changes made by the Children Act 1989.

5. Re-registration of birth where parents not married

Section 10A of the Births and Deaths Registration Act 1953, as substituted by s 25 of the Family Reform Act 1987, provides for the father's name to be recorded in cases where the birth of a child, whose father and mother were not married to each other at the time of the birth, was registered but no person has been shown as the father of the child. The re-registration will be effected:

(a) at the joint request of the mother and that person; or

(b) at the request of the mother on production of—

  (i) a declaration in the prescribed form (Form 2; see page 62), made by the mother stating that that person is the father of the child; and

  (ii) a statutory declaration made by that person stating himself to be the father of the child; or

(c) at the request of that person on production of—

8

    (i) a declaration in the prescribed form (Form 5; see page 64), stating himself to be the father of the child; and

    (ii) a statutory declaration made by the mother stating that that person is the father of the child; or

(d) at the request of the mother or that person (which must in either case be made in writing) on production of—

    (i) a certified copy of a relevant order (for the meaning of "relevant order" see page 8 above); and

    (ii) if the child has attained the age of sixteen, the written consent of the child to the registration of that person as his father.

Section 10A, however, provides that "No birth shall be re-registered under this section except in the prescribed form and with the authority of the Registrar General. Regulation 17 of the Registration of Births and Deaths Regulations 1987 sets out the procedure to be followed in cases of re-registrations of births of children whose parents are not married to each other.

The Children Act 1989, Sch 12 para 6, although not in force at January 1990, provides for ss 10 and 10A of the 1953 Act to be amended as follows:

'(2) In sections 10(1) and 10A(1) for paragraph (d) there shall be substituted—

"(d) at the request of the mother or that person on production of—

    (i) a copy of a parental responsibility agreement made between them in relation to the child; and

    (ii) a declaration in the prescribed form by the person making the request stating that the agreement was made in compliance with section 4 of the Children Act 1989 and has not been brought to an end by an order of a court; or

(e) at the request of the mother or that person on production of—

    (i) a certified copy of an order under section 4 of the Children Act 1989 giving that person responsibility for the child; and

9

    (ii) a declaration in the prescribed form by the person making the request stating that the order has not been brought to an end by an order of a court; or

(f) at the request of the mother or that person on production of—

    (i) a certified copy of an order under paragraph 1 of Schedule 1 to the Children Act 1989 which requires that person to make any financial provision for the child and which is not an order falling within paragraph 4(3) of that Schedule; and

    (ii) a declaration in the prescribed form by the person making the request stating that the order has not been discharged by an order of a court; or

(g) at the request of the mother or that person on production of—

    (i) a certified copy of any of the orders which are mentioned in subsection (1A) of this section which has been made in relation to the child; and

    (ii) a declaration in the prescribed form by the person making the request stating that the order has not been brought to an end or discharged by an order of a court."

(3) After sections 10(1) and 10A(1) there shall be inserted—

"(1A) The orders are—

(a) an order under section 4 of the Family Law Reform Act 1987 that that person shall have all the parental rights and duties with respect to the child;

(b) an order that that person shall have custody or care and control or legal custody of the child made under section 9 of the Guardianship of Minors Act 1971 at a time when such an order could only be made in favour of a parent;

(c) an order under section 9 or 11B of that Act which requires that person to make any financial provision in relation to the child;

(d) an order under section 4 of the Affiliation Proceedings Act 1957 naming that person as putative father of the child."

(4) In section 10(2) for the words "or (d)" there shall be substituted "to (g)".

(5) In section 10(3) for the words from " 'relevant order' " to the end there shall be substituted " 'parental responsibility agreement' has the same meaning as in the Children Act 1989".

(6) In section 10A(2) in paragraphs (b) and (c) for the words "paragraph (d)" in both places where they occur there shall be substituted "any of paragraphs (d) to (g)".'

6. Re-registration of births of legitimated persons

Section 14 of the Births and Deaths Registration Act 1953, as amended by the Legitimacy Act 1976 Sch 1 paragraph 6, permits the re-registration of the births of persons recognised by English law as having become legitimated by the subsequent marriage of their parents.

Section 9(1) of the Legitimacy Act 1976 makes it a duty of the parent of a legitimated person or, in the case where re-registration can be effected on information furnished by one parent and one of the parents is dead, of the surviving parent, to furnish to the Registrar General information with a view to obtaining the re-registration of the birth of that person within three months after the date of the marriage by virtue of which he was legitimated.

By virtue of s 9(3) of the Legitimacy Act 1976, any parent who fails to give information as required by s 9 will be liable, on summary conviction, to a fine.

The procedure for the re-registration of births of legitimated persons is set out in the Registration of Births and Deaths Regulations 1987 Part V Regulations 19 to 26. These regulations provide as follows:

"Attendance and particulars on re-registration

19. Where under section 14(1) of the Act the Registrar General authorises the re-registration of the birth of a legitimated person—

   (a) except where Regulation 21 or 23 applies, and subject to section 14(2) of the Act (personal attendance as required by the Registrar General), a parent of the legitimated person shall attend personally at the office of the relevant registrar for re-registration of the birth within such time as the Registrar General may direct;

(b) Regulation 7(2) shall apply as to the particulars to be recorded in respect of the parents except that—

    (i) in space 6 of form 1, the occupation of the father need not be recorded as at both the date of birth and the date of the entry,

    (ii) in space 7 of form 1, the surname to be recorded in respect of the mother of the child shall be her surname immediately after her marriage to the father, and

    (iii) in space 9(b) of form 1, the surname (if any) to be entered shall be that in which the mother contracted her most recent marriage prior to re-registration.

Re-registration where parent attends

20.—(1) Where the parent attends personally at the office of the relevant registrar for re-registration, the registrar shall show or read to the parent the particulars entered in the Registrar General's authority.

(2) If it appears that there is any error or omission in those particulars the registrar shall correct it in such manner as the Registrar General may direct.

(3) The registrar shall then in the presence of the parent—

(a) copy the particulars recorded in the spaces of the authority into the corresponding spaces of form 1 so however that if any particular has been corrected in pursuance of paragraph (2) he shall enter only the particulars as corrected, omitting any incorrect particular which has been struck out;

(b) enter in space 12 of form 1 the qualification of the informant as "father" or "mother", as the case may be, and call upon the parent to verify the particulars as entered and to sign the entry in space 14;

(c) enter in space 15 of form 1 the date on which the entry is made and add the words "On the authority of the Registrar General";

(d) sign the entry in space 16 of form 1 and add his official description.

Making of declaration where parent does not attend

21.—(1) Instead of attending personally at the office of the relevant registrar, a parent may with the written consent of the Registrar General verify the particulars required on re-registration in accordance with the following provisions of this Regulation.

(2) A parent who is in England or Wales may verify the particulars by making and signing before any registrar other than the relevant registrar a declaration of the particulars on an approved form.

(3) Any such declaration shall be attested by the registrar before whom it is made and sent by him to the relevant registrar.

(4) A parent who is not in England or Wales may verify the particulars by making and signing before a relevant authority, and sending to the Registrar General, a declaration of the particulars on an approved form.

(5) In paragraph (4) "relevant authority" means—

(a) in the case of a parent who is in Scotland, Northern Ireland, the Isle of Man, the Channel Islands or any part of the Commonwealth outside the British Islands or who is in the Irish Republic, a notary public and any other person who, in the place where the declaration is made, is authorised to administer oaths;

(b) in the case of a parent to whom sub-paragraph (a) above does not apply (and who is outside England and Wales), one of Her Majesty's consular officers, a notary public and any other person who, in the place where the declaration is made, is authorised to administer oaths so however that a declaration made otherwise than before a consular officer shall be authenticated by such an officer if the Registrar General so requires;

(c) in the case of a parent who is a member of Her Majesty's Forces and who is not in the United Kingdom, any officer who holds a rank not below that of Lieutenant-Commander, Major or Squadron-Leader.

Re-registration in pursuance of declaration

22. On receiving the Registrar General's authority to re-register a birth together with his consent as to verification and the declaration made for the purposes of Regulation 21, the relevant registrar shall—

(a) copy the particulars recorded in the spaces of the declaration into the corresponding spaces of form 1;

(b) enter in space 12 of form 1 the qualification of the informant as "father" or "mother", as the case may be;

(c) enter in space 14 of form 1 the name of the declarant in the form in which he signed the declaration and add the words "by declaration dated ......", inserting the date on which the declaration was made and signed;

(d) complete the entry as provided in regulation 20(3)(c) and (d).

Re-registration where particulars not verified by parent

23. Where, in a case to which any of the provisos to section 14(1) applies, the Registrar General authorises the relevant registrar to re-register the birth of a legitimated person notwithstanding that the particulars to be registered have not been verified by either parent, the registrar shall—

(a) copy the particulars recorded in the spaces of the authority into the corresponding spaces of form 1;

(b) enter in space 14 the words "On the authority of the Registrar General" without any further entry in that space;

(c) enter in space 15 the date on which the entry is made and sign the entry in space 16, adding his official description.

Noting of previous entry

24. Where the birth of a legitimated person is re-registered in accordance with Regulation 20, 22 or 23 the superintendent registrar or registrar having custody of the register in which the birth was previously registered shall, when so directed by the Registrar General, note in the margin of the previous entry the words "Re-registered under section 14 of the Births and Deaths Registration Act 1953, on ......", inserting the date of the re-registration.

Certified copies of re-registered entries

25. Where an application is made to a superintendent registrar or registrar for a certified copy of the entry of the birth of a legitimated person whose birth has been re-registered in a register in his custody—

(a) he shall supply a certified copy of the entry of re-registration;

(b) a certified copy of the superseded entry shall not be supplied except with the authority of the Registrar General.

Re-registration where person born at sea

26.—(1) Where under section 14(1) of the Act the Registrar General authorises the re-registration of the birth of a legitimated person who was born at sea and whose birth was included in a return sent to the Registrar General—

(a) a parent of the legitimated person shall verify the particulars required on re-registration by making and signing on an approved form a declaration of those particulars before a registrar or a relevant authority as defined in Regulation 21(5);

(b) the parent shall send the declaration to the Registrar General.

(2) In relation to any case to which this Regulation applies, section 14(1) of the Act shall apply with the modification that a person deputed for the purpose by the Registrar General shall on receiving the Registrar General's authority, together with the declaration made by the parent under paragraph (1), effect re-registration by—

(a) making the entry in a register to be kept at the General Register Office in form 7, copying the particulars recorded in the spaces of the authority into the corresponding spaces of the form;

(b) noting in the margin of any previous record of the birth in the custody of the Registrar General the words "Re-registered under section 14 of the Births and Deaths Registration Act 1953, on ......", inserting the date of re-registration; and

(c) sending a copy of the previous record, including a copy of the marginal note certified under the seal of the General Register Office, to the authority from whom that record was received by the Registrar General."

7. Re-registration after declaration of parentage

Section 56 of the Family Law Act 1986, as substituted by s 22 of the Family Law Reform Act 1987, provides for the court to make a declaration of parentage, legitimacy or legitimation. The new s 56 enables an application to be made by any person for a declaration:

(a) that a person named in the application is or was the applicant's parent; or

(b) that the applicant is the legitimate child of his parents.

Any person may also apply to the court for one (or for one or the other) of the following declarations:

(a) a declaration that he has become a legitimated person;

(b) a declaration that he has not become a legitimated person.

Section 23 of the Family Law Reform Act 1987 replaces references to blood tests and blood samples in the Family Law Reform Act 1969 by the terms "scientific tests" and "bodily samples". Under this new section the court may, either of its own motion or on an application by any party to the proceedings, give a direction:

(a) for the use of scientific tests to ascertain whether such tests show that a party to the proceedings is or is not the father or mother of that person; and

(b) for the taking, within a period specified in the direction, of bodily samples from all or any of the following, namely the applicant; any party who is alleged to be the father or mother of the applicant; and any other party to the proceedings.

"Bodily samples" is defined as meaning a sample of bodily fluid or bodily tissue; and "scientific tests" as tests carried out under the Act and made with the object of ascertaining the inheritable characteristics of bodily fluids or bodily tissues.

Where a declaration is made on an application under s 56(1) above, the prescribed officer of the court must notify the Registrar General of the making of that declaration; see s 56(4), as substituted by s 22 of the Family Law Reform Act 1987.

Section 14A of the Births and Deaths Registration Act 1953, inserted by s 26 of the Family Law Reform Act 1987, provides that where, in the case of a person whose birth has been registered in England and Wales

(a) the Registrar General receives, by virtue of s 56(4) of the Family Law Act 1986, a notification of the making of a declaration of parentage in respect of that person; and

(b) it appears to him that the birth of that person should be re-registered,

he shall authorise the re-registration of that person's birth, and the re-registration shall be effected in such manner and at such place as may be prescribed.

Re-registration under any of the above provisions will probably result in the change of the person's surname as recorded in the original registration.

Note: With regard to the registration of births in Wales, the prescribed forms are those set out in The Registration of Births and Deaths (Welsh Language) Regulations 1987 (SI 1987 No 2089).

Chapter 3

Changing a child's name

A child is not competent to change his name by his own motion; see *Re T (otherwise H) (An Infant)* (1963). But a child may acquire a name, particularly a surname, not registered at birth, as his surname involuntarily. A child is assumed to have the same name as that of the parent with whom he lives and upon whom he is dependent. If, therefore, the parent has changed his or her name, for example, on re-marriage or cohabitation, the likelihood is that in due course the child will involuntarily become known by the same surname as that of his parent. It should however be stressed that a parent who has the *de facto* custody of a child is not permitted to take any steps which would result in the child's name being changed without the consent of the other parent.

1. Changing a child's name where there are pending proceedings

In the case of proceedings for divorce, nullity of marriage or a decree of judicial separation, the Matrimonial Causes Rules 1977 Rule 92(8) provides that:

"Unless otherwise directed, any order giving a parent custody or care and control of a child shall provide that no steps (other than the institution of proceedings in any court) be taken by that parent which would result in the child being known by a new surname before he or she attains the age of 18 years or, being a female, marries before that age, except with the leave of a judge or the consent in writing of the other parent."

When the Children Act 1989 comes into force, by virtue of s 13 of that Act, where a residence order in respect of a child is in force, no person may cause the child to be known by a new surname without either the written consent of every person who has parental responsibility for the child, or the leave of the court.

Where the court has granted leave, or the other parent has given his/her consent to a child's surname being changed, it may be desirable to effect the change by deed poll and if it is intended that the deed poll should be enrolled, the requirements of the Enrolments of Deeds (Change of Name) Regulation 1983 (SI 1983 No 680) and the Practice Direction *Minors: Change of Surname: Parental Consent* (1977) will have to be complied with. See further pages 40–43. It is not, however, essential to execute a deed poll, nor for a deed poll, if effected, to be enrolled.

2. Disagreements between parents

In any pending proceedings where the court is concerned with a child, unless the other parent consents, a child's name may not be changed unilaterally by the parent having custody. The parent who is desirous of changing the child's name must apply to the court, by way of a summons in the High Court and a notice of application in the county court, supported by an affidavit setting out the grounds which are relied upon for the order sought.

In deciding such an application, the court, as in all other disputes relating to children, must have regard to the welfare and interest of the child. In decided cases before the Guardianship of Minors Act 1971 and the Guardianship Act 1973, the courts applied that principle. The following cases illustrate it.

Re T (otherwise H) (An Infant) (1963): on divorce the mother had been granted the custody of the child. She remarried and acquired her second husband's surname. Without any communication to the natural father of the child, she executed a deed poll purporting to change the child's surname to that of her second husband. When the father discovered the change he objected and applied to the court for the child to be warded and for the deed poll to be cancelled, or that a deed poll be ordered to be registered which would change the child's surname back to that of his natural father. It was held that a child of tender years could not of its own motion change his or her surname, as a change of name involved a conscious decision to change the name. Where there had been a divorce and custody had been granted to the mother this did not deprive the father of his rights and obligations in respect of the child. Further, Buckley J said ([1963] Ch at page 242):

> "In the case of a divided family of this sort it is always one of the aims of the court to maintain the child's contact, respect and affection with and for both parents so far as the circumstances will permit. But to deprive the child of her father's surname, in my judgement, is something which is not in the best interest of the child because, I think, it is injurious to the link between the father and the child to suggest to the child that there is some reason why it is desirable that she should be called by some name other than her father's name. The fact that there has been a divorce and that the father was the person against whom the decree was granted is an insufficient view. For these reasons, in my judgement, not only was the infant's mother incompetent to take a step on behalf of the infant which was of a kind calculated to have quite far-reaching effects upon the child but also, in my view, it was a step which was not in the interests of the infant and one which the court ought not to assist in any way."

In *J* v *C* (1970) (the case did not concern the change of name of the child), Lord MacDermott, when construing the meaning of the words ". . . shall regard the welfare of the infant as the first and paramount consideration", said ([1970] AC at page 710):

> "I think they connote a process whereby, when all the relevant facts, relationships, claims and wishes of the parents, choices and other circumstances are taken into account and weighed, the course to be followed will be that which is most in the interest of the child's welfare."

In *Y* v *Y (Child: Surname)* (1973), on divorce the custody of the two children of the family, both girls, had been committed to the mother in 1964. The following summer the mother stopped all access of the children to the father. In January 1965, the mother re-married and in July 1965, without consulting the father, she registered the children on the school register by the surname of her second husband. When the father discovered the change in the surname of his children he issued a summons asking, amongst other orders, for an order that the children should assume their former surname. When the matter came for consideration before Latey J the girls were aged thirteen and nine. It was held that an order for custody does not entitle the mother unilaterally to change a child's surname, as to do so would infringe the father's rights as natural guardian; nor is the father entitled unilaterally to cause a child's name to be changed as to do so would be to affect the rights of the mother as custodian. Where the court had become seised of the matters affecting children, a parent who wishes to take some step importantly affecting a child, such as a change of surname, the parent should seek the decision of the court. In the particular circumstances of the case, whatever the court's decision might have been in 1965, the court had to decide the matter after a lapse of some four years in a way which was in the best interests of the children. To change the older child's surname so that it reverted to that of her natural father would cause her acute embarrassment, and although the same did not apply to the younger child, it was plain that both children should have the same name.

Matters relating to the custody and the upbringing of a child are governed by the provisions of the Guardianship of Minors Act 1971 and the Guardianship Act 1973. Section 1 of the 1971 Act provides that where in any proceedings before any court:

" (a) the custody or upbringing of a child; or

   (b) the administration of any property belonging to or held on trust for a child, or the application of the income thereof,

is in question, the court, in deciding that question, shall regard the welfare of the child as the first and paramount consideration, and shall not take into consideration whether from any other point of view the claim of the father in respect of such legal custody, upbringing, administration or application is superior to that of the mother, or the claim of the mother is superior to that of the father."

Under the 1973 Act the mother is to have the same rights and authority as the law allows to a father, and the rights and authority of the mother and the father shall be equal and be exercisable by either without the other. The welfare principle is therefore the first and paramount consideration upon which the court's decision will be determined, and is re-enacted in s 1 Children Act 1989 (not in force at January 1990). The following more recent cases further illustrate the application of the principle by the courts:

In *Re D (Minors) (Adoption by Parent)* (1973), although the case concerned adoption proceedings, one of the objects of the adoption application was to give the children the surname of the mother's second husband. On this particular issue it was held that this could not by itself be a legitimate ground for adoption, nor would it generally be in the interest of the children.

In *Re WG* (1976), the parents of a little girl divorced on the ground of the father's adultery. The mother was granted custody and the father reasonable access. The mother re-married, as did the father. The father went to work in Singapore in May 1973 and thereafter he had no contact with the child. When the child started at school the mother was urged to change the child's name to that of her second husband. Faulks J took the view that it was in the child's best interest that her name should be changed, and gave leave for a deed poll to be registered. On appeal, Cairn LJ, having referred to the Practice Direction by the Master of the Rolls *Enrolment of Deeds Poll* (1969) and the Matrimonial Causes Rules 1974 r 92(8) said:

"that the headmistresses were quoted as saying (*inter alia*) that it would be more convenient for administrative reasons that L should be known by the mother's present name. While his Lordship had no doubt that there was administrative convenience from the school's point of view in having the same surname as the people with whom

22

L was living, it was wrong to attach too much importance to considerations in connection with schooling as against the longer term interests of L. It was, of course, important to bear in mind all the way through that it was the paramount interests of the child with which their Lordships were concerned. It had not been suggested on either side here that the court should approach the decision in the case from any other point of view. But his Lordship thought it important that it should be realised that the mere fact that there had been a divorce, that the mother had re-married and had custody of the child, and had a name different from that of the child, was not a sufficient reason for the changing of the child's surname. The court recognised the importance of maintaining a link with the father, unless he had ceased to have an interest in the child or there were some grounds—having regard to his character and behaviour—which made it undesirable for him to have access to the child at all. It must greatly tend to create difficulties in the relation between father and a child if the child ceased to bear the father's name— especially if, as here, the child had come to address her step-father as 'daddy' and refer to her father as 'old daddy'".

The appeal was allowed and the mother's application dismissed.

Contrast, however, the case of *R* v *R (Child: Surname)* (1978) where the mother had changed the child's name to that of her second husband for convenience. Ormrod LJ said:

"Rule 92(8) of the Matrimonial Causes (Amendment) Rules 1974, the new rule about changing names, has been drawn in a wider sense than the draftsman intended. I remember that at the time it was directed to preventing parents with custody or care and control orders changing children's names by deed poll or by some other formal means, but unfortunately, it now seems to be causing a great deal of trouble and difficulty to school authorities and to children and the very last thing that any rule of this court is intended to do is to embarrass children."

See also the case of *D* v *B (Surname: Birth Registration)* (1979) below.

In *L* v *F* (1978) the mother of two children aged three and four wished to change their surname to that of their step-father. The natural father objected. The mother applied to the court for leave to change their name. Latey J considered the two apparently irreconcilable decisions of the court on the approach to be adopted—on the one hand the decisions of the Court of Appeal in the cases of *R* v *R* *(Child: Surname)* (1978) and *D* v *B* *(Surname: Birth Registration)* (see below); and on the other hand the decisions in cases like *Re WG* (see above), the Practice Direction *Minors: Change of Surname: Parental Consent* (1977) (see page 41) and the Matrimonial Causes Rules 1977 r 92(8). He held that the question of change of name affected the best interests and psychological welfare of the children. In the circumstances it would be beneficial to the children to maintain their contact and relationship with their natural father. The mother's application was refused.

In *Crick* v *Crick* (1977), the mother, without being aware of the prohibition relating to change of a child's name, registered her children at school with the name Dell. The children were aware of their true surname but were not concerned about the use of this new name. The court amended the custody order to provide that the mother did not have to revert to the surname of Crick.

In *D* v *B* *(Surname: Birth Registration)* (1979), the mother had changed her surname by deed poll, and on the birth of her child registered the child's name in her assumed name. On the issue of the change of name, Ormrod LJ adopted the recommendation of the Official Solicitor that in the circumstances it was not in the interest of the child to be called by his father's surname as this would cause the child embarrassment when he attended school and would cause him distress in so far as he would be the only one in the family with a different surname. It was further stated that "what matters is whether the child identifies with the father in human terms".

In *W* v *A*, the parents had separated in 1971 when the mother left the husband with the two children aged three and one. A joint custody order was made, with care and control to the mother and reasonable access to the father. In 1974 the marriage was dissolved. Both parents then re-married. The mother had one child by her second husband

24

and the father had two children. The mother applied for leave for the children to be removed permanently to Australia. Leave was granted, subject to the mother's undertaking that the children would continue to be known by their natural father's surname. The mother appealed. The court held that in all matters concerning the future of a child, whether it be custody, access, education or change of name, the court should have regard to the welfare of the child as the first and paramount consideration as required by the Guardianship of Minors Act 1971 s 1:

> "It is a matter for the discretion of the individual judge hearing the case, seeing the parents, possibly seeing the children, to decide whether or not it is in the interests of the child in the particular circumstances of the case that his surname should or should not be changed; and the judge will take into account all the circumstances of the case, including no doubt where appropriate, any embarrassment which may be caused to the child by not changing his name and, on the other hand, the long term interests of the child, the importance of maintaining the child's links with his paternal family and the probable stability or otherwise of the mother's re-marriage. I only mention those as typical examples of the kind of considerations which arise in these cases, but the judge will take into account all the relevant circumstances in the particular case before him" (*per* Dunn LJ [1981] Fam at page 21).

In *R* v *R (Child: Surname)* (1982), the parents' marriage was dissolved in 1980. The custody of the only child, aged seven, was committed to the mother with reasonable access to the father. The mother re-married. The mother permitted the child to be known by her second husband's surname and registered her at school in that name. The child was aware of her true surname. On discovering the change in name, the child's natural father raised objections and the mother then applied for a decision by the court. The county court judge decided that it would not be in the best interest of the child to forbid the use of the mother's new surname and directed that the child may continue to be known at school and to her friends and companions as Donna T. The judge further ordered that the mother forthwith take all necessary steps to register the child for medical purposes as "Donna R (otherwise T)". The father appealed. His appeal was dismissed because the situation had become irreversible and the order made was in the best interests of the child.

It will be observed from these decisions that there is no hard and fast rule when it is intended to change a child's surname. Every case turns on its own facts, but in every case the court will apply the "welfare principle".

The Guardianship of Minors Act 1971 and the Guardianship Act 1973 will be repealed when the Children Act 1989 (which is not in force at January 1990) takes effect. The new Act provides that where a residence order, that is an order settling the arrangements to be made as to the person with whom a child is to live, is in force, no person may cause the child to be known by a new surname without either the written consent of every person who has parental responsibility for the child, or leave of the court.

If a disagreement arises or may arise with respect to a change of a child's surname, application may be made for a "specific issue order", that is, an order giving directions for the purpose of determining the specific question which has arisen or may arise, in connection with any aspect of parental responsibility for a child.

The determination of any such application to the court concerns the upbringing of the child, and the welfare principle laid down in s 1 of the Act will therefore be applied; that is, the child's welfare will be the court's paramount consideration. Furthermore, the court will make an order only if it is satisfied that the order will positively contribute to the child's welfare (s 1(5)).

When applying the welfare principle to a dispute involving a change in the child's name, the court will undoubtedly consider the matters set out in s 3(1) Children Act 1989, namely:

(a) the ascertainable wishes and feelings of the child concerned (considered in the light of his age and understanding);

(b) his physical, emotional and educational needs;

(c) the likely effect on him of any change in his circumstances;

(d) his age, sex, background and any characteristics of his which the court considers relevant;

(e) any harm which he has suffered or is at risk of suffering.

Thus, although the provisions of the Guardianship of Minors Act 1971 and the Guardianship Act 1973 will be repealed, the cases cited in this chapter will continue to provide guidance because the "welfare principle" will remain the basis upon which the court must make its decision.

3. Children born out of wedlock

The case of a child whose parents are not married to each other must be considered in the light of the Family Law Reform Act 1987, under which the mother of a child born out of wedlock continues to have exclusive parental rights and duties with respect to that child.

Section 4 of the Act, however, makes provision in such cases for the father of the child to apply for an order that he should have all the parental rights and duties in respect of the child; and the court may make an order that he shall have those rights and duties jointly with the mother of the child or, if the mother is dead, jointly with any guardian of the child appointed under the Guardianship of Minors Act 1971. In such cases, re-registration will follow the procedure set out on pages 8 to 11). See also pages 28 to 29 for the changes made by the Children Act 1989.

Where there is a dispute regarding any change in the child's name, application should be made to the court for its direction. In determining the application, the court will apply the "welfare principle" under s 1 Guardianship of Minors Act 1971, or, when in force, s 1 Children Act 1989 (see above).

4. Disagreements where there are no pending proceedings

Section 1(3) of the Guardianship Act 1973, as amended by s 5 of the Family Law Reform Act 1987, now provides as follows:

"(3) Subject to subsection (3A) below where a child's father and mother disagree on any question affecting his welfare, either of them may apply to the court for its direction, and (subject to subsection (4) below) the court may make such order regarding the matters in difference as it may think proper.

(3A) Where a child's father and mother were not married to each other at the time of his birth, subsection (3) above does not apply unless—

(a) an order is in force under section 4 of the Family Law Reform Act 1987 giving the father all the parental rights and duties with respect to the child; or

(b) the father has a right to custody, legal or actual or care and control of the child by virtue of an order made under any other enactment."

Thus, under the provisions of subs (3), where the parents of the child are married to each other, then in the event of any disagreement between them affecting the welfare of the child, either may apply to the court for directions. It appears from all the earlier decisions referred to above that any dispute regarding the surname of the child comes within the provisions of s 1 of the Guardianship of Minors Act 1971 and consequently under s 1(3) of the Guardianship Act 1973.

The courts having jurisdiction to entertain such an application are the High Court, county courts and magistrates' courts authorised to hear those applications.

In the case of disagreements where the child's mother and father are not married to each other, it appears from the provisions of subs (3A) that the application for directions cannot be made unless the father has applied for and obtained an order in his favour granting him parental rights and duties with respect to the child; or the father has a right to custody or care and control of the child under an order made under any other statute.

The provisions of ss 4 and 5 will be repealed when the Children Act 1989 comes into force. Thereafter, in the event of a dispute between parents relating to the change of a child's surname, application may be made to the court for a s 8 order—that is, a "specific issue order" (see pages 26 to 27).

It should be noted that where a child's father is not married to the mother at the time of the child's birth, s 2(2) Children Act 1989 provides that:

(a) the mother shall have parental responsibility for the child;

(b) the father shall not have parental responsibility for the child unless he acquires it in accordance with the provisions of the Act.

Acquisition of parental responsibility by the father may be obtained under s 4 in one of two ways:

(a) by making an application to the court for an order that he shall have parental responsibility; or

(b) he and the mother may by consent make a parental responsibility agreement providing for the father to have parental responsibility for the child. The parental responsibility agreement must be in a prescribed form.

5. Where the parents agree

Where there is an agreement between the parents of a child, or where one of the parents is dead or cannot be found, the child's name may be changed by deed poll, which may be enrolled under s 133 Supreme Court Act 1981 and the Enrolment of Deeds (Change of Names) Regulations 1983 (SI 1983 No 680; see page 32). This procedure, however, is not essential. The child's name may alternatively be changed by a statutory declaration. The statutory declaration may be made before a solicitor, when a fee will be payable; or before a magistrate when there is a nominal statutory fee for witnessing the declaration, but this is often waived.

For the relevant forms, see pages 68, 69, 71, 74, 75, 77 and 79.

Chapter 4

Change of name by deed poll

In England and Wales any person may legally change his name to whatever he chooses by simple assumption and usage so long as the intention in so doing is not fraudulent. Change by usage and reputation is the *only* way in which a name can be changed.

There is no specific legal requirement or procedure which needs to be adopted, save in the case of minors, as set out in Chapter 3. Good examples of the acquisition of a name by usage and reputation are the cases of *R* v *Billinghurst (Inhabitants)* (1814) and *Dancer* v *Dancer* (1949).

A change of name by deed poll and by the various other ways referred to later are merely ways of *evidencing* and *advertising* the change. In certain instances such evidence may be necessary; for example where a person is a member of a profession, the rules applicable to the governing body of the profession may require the change to be evidenced by deed poll or in some other way. In this chapter a change of name as evidenced by deed poll and the enrolment of the deed will be discussed. The other ways of effecting the change will be dealt with later in the text.

1. The deed poll

The most common method of evidencing a change of name is by executing a deed poll and having it witnessed. Standard forms for this are obtainable from law stationers, and specimen forms are set out on pages 66 to 77.

Where it is intended to change a child's name, the form differs depending on whether the child is under sixteen or over sixteen. In the case of a child under sixteen, provided the parents agree, or one of them is dead or cannot be found, the change of name can be evidenced in the same way as by an adult executing a deed poll, but the deed will be executed by the parent on behalf of the child.

Where the child is over sixteen he may execute the deed on his own behalf subject to the consent of his parents, or the deed may be executed on his behalf by his parents but it must be endorsed with his consent. Again, specimen forms are shown on pages 68, 69, 71, 74–77.

When duly executed and attested the deed may be enrolled in the Central Office of the Supreme Court. In order to apply for a deed poll to be enrolled the conditions laid down in the Enrolment of Deeds (Change of Name) Regulations 1983 (SI 1983 No 680) must be complied with. These are set out at pages 32 to 33. There is no legal provision which requires that a deed poll of change of name *must* be enrolled. An application to enrol is entirely discretionary. The enrolment of a deed poll does not make the change of name any more legally effective than the execution of the deed itself. The purpose and advantages of enrolling the deed are that it provides certainty, safe custody, availability of copies when required, and the change of name is advertised in the *London Gazette*. There is no time limit within which a deed poll may be enrolled.

A change of name which has been evidenced by deed poll may be changed again by another deed, or by any other means whether formal or informal. If a deed has been enrolled it may be cancelled. Where a dispute arises with respect to a change of name, for example between parents where a child's name has been changed by one parent unilaterally, as happened in *Re T (otherwise H) (An Infant)* (1963), the court to which an application is made may declare that the deed was ineffective to change the name.

An alien is now free to change his name like any other individual and may effect the change by deed poll or by any other means. If the change is effected by deed poll the deed may not be enrolled because the regulations mentioned above require that the applicant must be a British citizen or a Commonwealth citizen as defined by s 37(1) of the British Nationality Act 1981 (see page 34).

2. Enrolment of a deed poll

If it is desired to enrol the deed poll of change of name, the conditions of enrolment laid down in the Enrolment of Deeds (Change of Name) Regulations 1983 made by the Master of the Rolls under s 133(1) of the Supreme Court Act 1981 on 27 April 1983 (SI 1983 No 680) must be complied with. The regulations came into operation on 1 June 1983, and provide as follows:

"1. (1) These regulations may be cited as the Enrolment of Deeds (Change of Name) Regulations 1983, and shall come into operation on June 1, 1983.

(2) These Regulations shall govern the enrolment in the Central Office of the Supreme Court of deeds evidencing change of name.

2. (1) The applicant must be a Commonwealth citizen as defined in [s 37(1) of the British Nationality Act 1981]. If the applicant is a British citizen, a British Dependent Territories citizen or a British Overseas citizen, he must be described as such in the deed poll which must also specify the section of the Act under which the relevant citizenship was acquired. In all other cases, the applicant must be described as a Commonwealth citizen.

(2) The applicant must be described as single, married, widowed or divorced.

3. (1) As proof of the citizenship claimed in the deed poll, the applicant must produce:

(a) a certificate of birth; or

(b) a certificate of citizenship by registration or naturalisation or otherwise; or

(c) some other document evidencing such citizenship.

(2) In addition to the documents set out in the last preceding paragraph, an applicant who is married must:

(a) produce his certificate of marriage;

(b) show that notice of his intention to apply for the enrolment of the deed poll evidencing the change of name has been given to his spouse by delivery or by post to his spouse's last known address; and

32

(c) show that he has obtained the consent of his spouse to the proposed change of name or that there is good reason why such consent should be dispensed with.

4. The deed poll and the documents mentioned in Regulation 3 must be exhibited to a statutory declaration by a Commonwealth citizen who is a householder resident in the United Kingdom and who must in the statutory declaration declare that he is such. The declaration must state the period, which should not be less than ten years, during which the householder has known the applicant and must identify the applicant with the person referred to in the documents exhibited to the declaration.

5. If the applicant is resident outside the United Kingdom, evidence will be required that such residence is not intended to be permanent, and the applicant may be required to produce a certificate by a solicitor as to the nature and probable duration of such residence.

6. The deed poll must be signed by the applicant in both his old and new names.

7. (1) Upon enrolment the deed poll shall be advertised in the London Gazette by the clerk in charge for the time being of the Filing and Record Department of the Central Office of the Supreme Court.

(2) The expense of the advertisement required by paragraph (1) shall be borne by the applicant, and shall be paid by him to the clerk in charge when the deed is enrolled."

[Regulation 8 is set out on pages 40 to 41.]

There is no stamp duty payable on the deed itself. If the deed is to be enrolled the following fees are payable:

Advertisement Fee:	£40.25
Copy of Gazette and Postage:	£ 1.15
Enrolment Fee:	£ 2.25
Total Fees:	£43.65

The total fees are payable by two cheques, one for £2.25, and the other for £41.40. The cheques must be made payable to Her Majesty's Paymaster-General. Note that cheques *by post* from individuals are not accepted. If personal attendance is made, a banker's card will need to be produced. If it is proposed to deal with the application by post a Postal Order, made out as set out above, would be acceptable.

3. Definitions

(a) Commonwealth citizen

The Regulations require that the applicant must be a Commonwealth citizen within the meaning of the British Nationality Act 1981 s 37(1). That section defines the term as follows:

"Every person who—

(a) under this Act is a British citizen, a British Dependent Territories citizen, a British Overseas citizen or a British subject; or

(b) under any enactment for the time being in force in any country mentioned in Schedule 3 is a citizen of that country."

The countries listed in Sch 3 whose citizens are Commonwealth citizens are:

Antigua and Barbuda	Mauritius
Australia	Nauru
The Bahamas	New Zealand
Bangladesh	Nigeria
Barbados	Papua New Guinea
Belize	Saint Lucia
Botswana	Saint Vincent and the Grenadines
Canada	Seychelles
Republic of Cyprus	Sierra Leone
Dominica	Singapore
Fiji	Solomon Islands
The Gambia	Sri Lanka
Ghana	Swaziland
Grenada	Tanzania
Guyana	Tonga
India	Trinidad and Tobago
Jamaica	Tuvalu
Kenya	Uganda
Kiribati	Vanuatu
Lesotho	Western Samoa
Malawi	Zambia
Malaysia	Zimbabwe
Malta	

(b) British citizenship

British citizenship may be acquired in a number of ways under the British Nationality Act 1981.

By birth or adoption: Under s 1(1) of the 1981 Act a child born in the United Kingdom after the commencement of the Act will be a British citizen if at the time of his birth his father or mother is either a British citizen or is settled in the United Kingdom. Note however that:

   (i) a child born on a British aircraft or a ship will be a British citizen only if at least one of the parents was a British citizen at the time of the birth (BNA 1981 s 50(7));

 (ii) a child born in the United Kingdom whose mother or father is a diplomat will not be a British citizen (BNA 1981 s 50(4));

(iii) a person is settled in the United Kingdom if he or she is ordinarily resident in the United Kingdom without being under any restrictions on the length of time for which he may remain; BNA 1981 s 50(2). Section 50(5) provides that no one who is in breach of the immigration laws can be said to be ordinarily resident in the United Kingdom. Therefore a child born to such a person will not qualify to acquire British citizenship by birth under s 1(1).

Subsequent acquisition: The BNA 1981 provides for a child who is born in the United Kingdom when the Act came into force but who has not acquired British citizenship at birth to acquire it subsequently by registration. These cases are as follows:

   (i) if either of his parents subsequently becomes a British citizen or becomes settled in the United Kingdom and the child is under the age of eighteen years (s 1(3));

 (ii) if the child has remained in the United Kingdom for ten years since his birth without being absent for more than ninety days in any one year (s 1(4)). Where the child *has* remained absent for a period in excess of ninety days the Secretary of State has a discretion to disregard the excess;

(iii) under Sch 2 para 3, which provides that a person born in the United Kingdom or a dependent territory after the commencement shall be entitled on an application for registration to be registered if the following requirements are satisfied, namely:

- that he is and has always been stateless; and
- that on the date of the application he had attained the age of ten but was under the age of twenty-one; and
- that he was in the United Kingdom or a dependent territory (no matter which) at the beginning of the period of five years prior to the date of the application either in the United Kingdom or mostly in the United Kingdom and partly in the dependent territory but that he was absent from both for no more than 450 days. In special circumstances the Secretary of State has discretion to disregard any excess (BNA 1981 Sch 2 paras 3 and 6).

If a child is stateless then if either of his parents is a British Dependent Territories citizen, British Overseas citizen or a British citizen the child will acquire British citizenship (BNA 1981 Sch 2 para 1).

Where a child is adopted in the United Kingdom by a person who, at the date of the adoption, is a British citizen the child will acquire British citizenship. Where the adoption is by two persons jointly then it is sufficient if only one of the adopters is a British citizen. Note however that if both or either of them are settled in the United Kingdom this does not confer British citizenship on the adopted child.

A new-born baby found abandoned in the United Kingdom will acquire British citizenship (BNA 1981 s 1(2)).

By descent: A person born outside the United Kingdom after the commencement of BNA 1981 will be a British citizen if at the time of his birth his father or mother:

(i) is a British citizen by birth, adoption, registration or naturalisation; or

(ii) is a British citizen and is serving outside the United Kingdom in Crown service, the recruitment to which took place in the United Kingdom (BNA 1981 s 2(1));

(iii) is a British citizen and is serving outside the United Kingdom with any of the European Community institutions, the recruitment for which took place in any of the member states.

By registration: British citizenship by registration may be acquired by a minor, a person who is a British Dependent Territories citizen, a British Overseas citizen, a British subject under the BNA 1981 or a British protected person. The relevant provisions under the Act are ss 3 to 5, 7 to 9, 15, 19 and 20 to 22.

By naturalisation: Application for naturalisation can be made only by a person of full age and capacity and subject to the requirements set out in Sch 3 (ss 6 and 18).

(c) *British Dependent Territories citizenship*

A person may acquire British Dependent Territories citizenship by birth, adoption, descent, registration and naturalisation. The requirements are similar to those applicable to acquisition of British citizenship. The relevant provisions are set out in ss 15 to 25 of the BNA 1981.

(d) *British Overseas citizenship*

British Overseas citizens are those who were citizens of the United Kingdom and Colonies who are not British citizens or British Dependent Territories citizens. Under the BNA 1981 this form of citizenship will not perpetuate and the number will in due course diminish. The relevant provisions are ss 26 to 28 of the BNA 1981.

(e) *British subjects*

The provisions are set out in ss 30 to 33 of the BNA 1981. British subjects are:

(i) persons who were British subjects without citizenship by virtue of s 13 or 16 of the Act; or

(ii) alien women who had registered as British subjects under the British Nationality Act 1965;

(iii) certain former citizens of Eire who were British subjects prior to 1 January 1949.

Inquiries relating to citizenship and status generally should be addressed to the Home Office, Nationality Division, Lunar House, 40 Wellesley Road, Croydon, Surrey CR9 2BY.

Note that where the applicant is a British citizen, a British Dependent Territories citizen or a British Overseas citizen not only must he be described as such in the deed poll but the section of the Act under which the relevant citizenship was acquired must also be specified. In the case of Commonwealth citizens it is sufficient to refer to s 37(1) of the Act.

4. Affidavits

The Enrolment of Deeds (Change of Name) Regulations 1983, Regulation 3(2) requires that, on enrolling the deed, where the applicant is married the marriage certificate must be produced. Also, it must be shown that notice of intention to change the name has been given to the other spouse by delivery or by post, and that the other spouse has consented to the application or that there are grounds for dispensing with such consent. Evidence of these matters should be given on affidavit, which should:

(a) set out the reasons for the change of name;

(b) exhibit a copy of the marriage certificate;

(c) confirm that notice of the intention to apply for enrolment of the deed poll evidencing the change of name has been given to the other spouse, and state the manner in which such notice was given, eg by delivery or by post;

(d) state whether the other spouse has consented, refused to consent or failed to consent;

(e) if consent has been given the form of consent should be exhibited;

(f) if it is intended to apply for the consent to be dispensed with the affidavit should specifically apply for this and set out the grounds upon which the dispensation is sought. If dispensation is sought on the ground that the other spouse's whereabouts are not known the affidavit must set out all the relevant details including when, where and in what circumstances he/she was last seen, the last known address of his/her residence and employment, details of family who may be able to assist to trace the person and the steps which have been undertaken to trace his/her whereabouts;

(g) if the applicant is living with another, the name of the cohabitee must be given and whether the person is married, separated or divorced;

(h) if the applicant and/or the cohabitee have children from their relationship or from a previous marriage, particulars of the children, ie their names, dates of birth, residence, custody and other relevant facts, must be disclosed in the affidavit;

(i) where relevant, evidence as required by Regulation 5 (see page 33) as to residence outside the United Kingdom not intended to be permanent.

For a form of affidavit seeking dispensation from the requirement for a spouse's consent, see pages 74 to 75.

5. Procedural steps

When the deed poll has been executed in the appropriate form, the executed deed should be presented to the Filing and Record Department in Room 81 at the Royal Courts of Justice, Strand, London WC2. It must be accompanied, as appropriate, by passports; immigration documents if appropriate; certificate of registration or naturalisation or other document evidencing citizenship; birth certificate; statutory declaration by the householder if appropriate (see page 59 for forms); any necessary consents and affidavits; a draft of the *London Gazette* advertisement; and two cheques or postal orders (see page 33) in the appropriate sum.

A praecipe for the fee will be issued on acceptance of the documents, whereupon the appropriate fee should be paid and then the praecipe returned to the Department. The deed, endorsed with the certificate of enrolment and a copy of the *London Gazette* in which the advertisement appeared, will be forwarded by post to the person or his solicitors.

6. Change of name of a child by deed poll

(a) The deed poll

A child's name may be changed by deed poll either:

    (a) by the parents if they agree; or

    (b) with the leave of the court (see Chapter 3).

Although not essential, the deed poll may be enrolled in the High Court. Regulation 8 of the Enrolment of Deeds (Change of Name) Regulations 1983 (see below) makes provision for the enrolment of deeds in respect of minors. Enrolment does not give the deed any statutory force but it provides certainty, particularly regarding compliance with the necessary requirements, safe custody and the availability of copies when required.

In addition to the provisions of Regulation 8, the requirement for the consent of the other parent on the application by a parent to change the name of a child by enrolment of a deed poll, is governed by a Practice Direction issued with the approval of the Master of the Rolls. The Practice Direction (see below) supplements the regulation and must be read in conjunction with it.

Regulation 8 provides as follows:

"(1) The provisions of this regulation shall apply in relation to a deed poll evidencing the change of name of a minor notwithstanding anything in the foregoing regulations.

(2) The statutory declaration referred to in Regulation 4 must state the period during which the householder has known the minor and his parent or parents respectively.

(3) If the minor has attained the age of 16, the deed poll must either:

    (a) be signed by him in both his old and new names; or

    (b) be executed on his behalf by a parent or legal guardian of his, and be indorsed with the minor's signed and duly witnessed consent.

(4) If the minor is under the age of 16, the deed poll must be executed by a parent or legal guardian of his.

(5) The application for enrolment must be supported:
   (a) by an affidavit showing that the change of name is for the benefit of the minor and:
      (i) that the application is submitted by both his parents; or
      (ii) that it is submitted by one parent with the consent of the other; or
      (iii) that it is submitted by one parent without the consent of the other, or by some other person whose name and capacity are given, for reasons set out in the affidavit; and

   (b) by such other evidence, if any, as the Master of the Rolls may in the particular circumstances of the case require.

(6) In relation to a minor who is a child in respect of whom parental rights are vested in a local authority pursuant to section 3(1) of the Child Care Act 1980 by reason of the fact that his parents are dead and that he has no guardian or custodian, any reference in this Regulation to the legal guardian of the minor shall be construed as a reference to that local authority."

The Practice Direction *Minors: Change of Surname: Parental Consent* (1977) provides that:

"(1)(a) Where a parent has by any order of the High Court or county court been given custody or care and control of a child and applies to the Central Office, Filing Department, for the enrolment of a deed poll to change the surname of such child who is under the age of 18 years (unless in the case of a female, she is married below that age) the application must be supported by the production of the consent in writing of the other parent.

(b) In the absence of such consent, the application will be adjourned generally unless and until leave is given to change the surname in the proceedings in which the said order was made, and such leave is produced to the Central Office. ·

2(a) Where an application is made to the Central Office, Filing Department, by a parent who has not been given the custody or care and control of the child by any order of the High Court or the county court for the enrolment of a deed to change the surname of such child who is under the age of 18 years (unless in the case of a female, she is married below that age), leave of the court to enrol

41

such deed will be granted if the consent in writing of the other parent is produced or if the other parent is dead or beyond the seas or despite the exercise of reasonable diligence it has not been possible to find him or her or for other good reason.

(b) In the case of any doubt the Senior Master or in his absence the Practice Master, will refer the matter to the Master of the Rolls.

(c) In the absence of any of the conditions specified above, the Senior Master, or the Master of the Rolls, as the case may be, may refer the matter to the Official Solicitor for investigation and report."

(b) Consent

The Regulations and the Practice Direction read in conjunction clearly require that where there are no pending proceedings it is essential to obtain the written consent of the other parent, or to provide evidence to show that the other parent is dead, or beyond the seas or that, despite reasonable diligence, he/she cannot be found, or for other good reason.

It is not however clear whether, where the mother and father of a child are not married, the term "parent" includes the father. The Regulations do not specifically exclude a natural father. On the other hand there is no provision that requires that the child in such cases should bear the surname of his/her natural father.

However, having regard to the changes to be brought about by the Children Act 1989, it would be desirable to err on the side of caution and to obtain such consent.

(c) Benefit of the minor

Under Regulation 8 (5)(a) it must be shown that the change of name is for the benefit of the child, and evidence to this effect must be submitted by affidavit and supported by such other evidence as may be required by the Master of the Rolls. For a form of affidavit, see pages 75 to 77.

(d) Minor's age

In the case of a child under sixteen, the deed must be executed by the parents or guardian if it is to be accepted for enrolment. If the parental rights of the child are vested in the local authority, for example because the parents are dead, the local authority would be the appropriate guardian to make the application for an enrolment of the deed. In such cases the resolution by the local authority to change the child's name, and any other relevant circumstances in respect of the child which would show that it would be to his benefit to change his name, should be produced. The deed should be executed by an authorised local authority officer.

Where a child is over sixteen years of age:

(i) the parent or guardian may execute the deed, but the child's consent must be endorsed on the deed and witnessed (Regulation 8(3)); or

(ii) the child may execute his own deed but the application to enrol must be made by the parents or guardian and supported by affidavit.

In all cases, the householder's declaration must accompany the application. See pages 69 and 71 for forms.

Where a man intends to change his name and it is intended that the rest of the family should assume the same new name it is desirable to include particulars of his wife and the children in the deed to show clearly that the change applies to them as well. Where a child is over sixteen, his consent must be endorsed on the deed.

Chapter 5

Miscellaneous methods of changing a name

1. By reputation

A surname in common law is simply the name by which a person is generally known. If a person assumes a name, not for the purposes of fraud or deceit, but on a *bona fide* claim of right, a court of law has no power to control the action of such a person (*Cowley* v *Cowley* [1901] AC at page 458).

> "An adult can change his or her name at any time by assuming a new name by any means as a result of which he or she becomes customarily addressed by the new name. There is no magic in a deed poll. The effect of changing a name by deed poll, as has been seen, is merely to record the change in solemn form which will perpetuate the evidence of the change of name. But a change of name on the part of an adult must, in my judgement, involve a conscious decision on the part of the adult that he wishes to change his name and be generally known by his new name. An infant . . . is not competent to make such a decision. Certainly an infant of tender years cannot of its own motion change his or her surname" (*per* Buckley J in *Re T (otherwise H) (An Infant)* [1963] Ch 238 at pages 240 and 241).

Thus there is no need to enter into any formal legal procedure so long as the person is identified by his assumed name.

There may, however, be circumstances, such as when applying for a passport, which require evidence of the acquisition of the new name by reputation to be produced. To facilitate and ease the change various ways are employed to record it. The deed poll discussed in the earlier chapter is one of the methods which is very commonly used.

2. Advertisement

The change may be recorded by placing an advertisement in a local and or national paper renouncing the old name and recording the assumption of the new name. Frequently the advertisement is placed in the *London Gazette* (see page 77).

3. Declaration

The Statutory Declarations Act 1835 prescribes the form of declaration to be used. The declaration sets out the person's intention to change his name and records the intention to renounce, relinquish and abandon the old name and to adopt the new name. The declaration may be made before a person authorised to take oaths, or before the magistrates' court clerk. Specimen forms are set out at pages 70 and 71.

4. By notarial instrument

Where it is required that a change of name be recognised world-wide, the change of name can be effected by a notarial act together with a declaration of the intention to renounce the original name and an intention to adopt the new name. The statutory declaration is prepared by a notary public. The declaration will set out the particulars of the person's citizenship and then formally record the intention to renounce, relinquish and abandon the former name and to assume the new name. The declaration is made before the notary, who authenticates it and then records it in a register.

5. Marriage

On marriage it is usual for a woman to assume the surname of her husband, but it is neither obligatory nor required by law for her to do so. In recent years, with women entering the professions in increasing numbers, it is not uncommon for women to retain their maiden names.

Where, however, a woman on marriage has assumed her husband's name she will continue to retain it unless she ceases to use it by reputation (see above) and reverts to her maiden name or some other name: see *Cowley* v *Cowley* (1901); *Fendall* v *Goldsmid* (1877).

6. On confirmation

A Christian name given to a child on baptism may be changed on confirmation. The following passage from Coke's Institute 1.3a (1633) is cited for this proposition:

> "If a man be baptized by the name of Thomas, and, after, at his confirmation by the bishop, he is named John, he may purchase by the name of his confirmation".

Coke mentions in that passage the case of Sir Francis Gawdie, Chief Justice of the Common Plea, who was given the name of Thomas on baptism but took the name of Francis on confirmation.

Dr Burn in the 9th edition of his *Ecclesiastical Law* 80 questioned the accuracy of this view, but Phillimore (see *Phillimore's Ecclesiastical Law of the Church of England* 2nd Edition 517, 1895) was of the opinion that the *dictum* remained good law. Phillimore mentions cases in which the precedent was followed and there are also references in *Notes & Queries 4th Series* 6, 17 & 7 Series 2, 77.

In *Re Parrott* [1946] Ch 183 at page 186, Vaisey J approved the opinion of Phillimore, and held that there were only three possible ways in which the name given on baptism could be changed, namely:

> "first it may be assumed, by the omni-competence of an Act of Parliament as for example, the Baines Name Act 1907. Secondly at confirmation as explained in Phillimore's Ecclesiastical Law . . . A third method by which a Christian name may in a sense be altered is under the power to 'add' a name when the child is adopted; but the precise quality of such an added name is I think open to

some doubt, for no one can in strictness possess more than one Christian name, whether it consists of one word or of several, and this method may perhaps be regarded as anomalous".

7. By Act of Parliament

A Christian name and surname may be changed by an Act of Parliament, such as the Baines Name Act 1907, a private Act under which the original Christian name Raymond Hill was changed to Henry Rodd. It is unusual to use this method to change a name, but there may be instances where it is necessary to adopt it—for example, in the rare case where a will requires a change of name as a precondition of a gift. As to the procedure to be followed, see *Halsbury's Laws of England*, 4th Edition Vol 34 para 1320.

8. Royal licence

A name may be changed by royal licence. It is necessary to effect a change of surname in this way if it is intended to assume the arms of one family by another. The application must be made to the College of Arms for a petition in proper form, stating the grounds for the application and any other relevant matters. The petition is to be drawn by one of the officers of the arms and signed by the applicant. The application is submitted through the Home Secretary to the Sovereign.

The granting of the royal licence is discretionary. The Sovereign is advised by the Home Secretary, who obtains a report on the matter from the Garter King of Arms as representing the Earl Marshall. (See further *Halsbury's Laws of England*, 4th Edition Vol 35 874/875.)

9. The College of Arms

In addition to effecting a change of name by royal licence, the College of Arms, Queen Victoria Street, London EC4V 4BT also prepares and records changes of names by deed poll. The change of name is advertised in the *London*

Gazette. The College will keep a record of the deed. It is not necessary for a deed prepared by the College to be enrolled at the Central Office. As in the case of enrolment, a deed recorded with the College has the advantage that it is in safe custody and copies are available.

10. On adoption

On an application for an adoption order the applicants may apply for a change in the forenames of the child. If the application is granted the court will direct that the child is to adopt a new name. A certified copy of the entry will be entered on the Adopted Children's Register and the original entry in the Register of Births will be marked with the word "adopted" or "re-adopted" or as the case may be. See further s 50 Adoption Act 1976.

Chapter 6

Requirements of some of the professional bodies

Where a person is a member of a professional or other organisation, the governing body may have special requirements for recording changes of name. The rules of some bodies are given as an illustration and no more. It is suggested In the case of other organisations less formal evidence may be adequate. The requirements of the following professional bodies are given as an illustration and no more. It is suggested that where a person who is a member of a profession wishes to change his name, inquiry should be made to the governing body to ascertain the precise requirements which apply and the procedure to be adopted.

1. Solicitors

Pursuant to the Solicitors Act 1974, The Law Society maintains a roll which sets out the name by which the solicitor was known at the time of his/her admission as a solicitor. Any change in the entry in the roll can be made only in accordance with regulations made by the Master of the Rolls with the concurrence of the Lord Chancellor and the Lord Chief Justice under s 28 Solicitors Act 1974 as amended by s 8 and Sch 1 para 8 of the Administration of Justice Act 1985.

The regulations which are presently applicable were made on 17 January 1989 and came into effect on 1 February 1989. They are the Solicitors (Keeping of the Roll) Regulations

1989. Part IV, Regulations 12 to 15 deal with the change of name on the roll, and provide as follows:

"12. Where the name of a solicitor is changed in consequence:

(a) in the case of a woman, of marriage; or

(b) in the case of the acquisition of a title,

the Society makes the appropriate change in the roll upon production to the Society of the change which is satisfactory to the Society.

13. (a) An application by a Solicitor that his name be changed upon the roll in circumstances other than mentioned in Regulation 12 shall be made to the Society by way of Form KR5 or in a form to the like effect.

(b) The application shall be supported by a Deed Poll or statutory declaration by the applicant providing satisfactory evidence of the change of name.

14. Upon receipt of an application under Regulations 12 and 13 the Society shall:

(a) display in the Society's Hall and make public in such other manner as the Society thinks fit particulars of the applicant, the nature of his application, his present private and business address, the date of his admission and every address at which he formerly practised as a solicitor;

(b) Give notice of such particulars to any solicitor or firm with whom the applicant might in the opinion of the Society be confused if the proposed changes were made.

15. Any person aggrieved by the removal of his name from the roll or refusal by the Society to grant his application for removal of his name from the roll, or restoration of name to the roll or change of his name on the roll under these Regulations may, within 28 days of the notice of the Society's decision, appeal to the Master of the Rolls in accordance with the Regulations as Applications and Appeals to the Master of the Rolls 1964."

2. Opticians

The General Optical Council was set up by the Opticians Act 1950 and its duties include the maintaining of three registers for the registration of opticians. Entitlement to registration arises from qualification, and once qualified and registered, an optician may practise in the United Kingdom and some other countries.

Registration is renewed annually, and the General Optical Council (Regulation and Enrolment Rules) Order in Council 1977 (SI 1977 No 176), which has been amended by subsequent orders, sets out the procedure. These rules provide that each register must contain the full name of each registered optician, and that the optician must retain that registration by returning certain particulars and paying the requisite retention fee for each year, otherwise his name is erased from the register.

Rule 12 provides that a registered optician must notify the Council within one month of any change of name. Under Rule 15, the Registrar, on receipt of the information, has to satisfy himself by means of a statutory declaration or otherwise that the information is accurate. If so satisfied he will make the required alteration.

If the alteration is required by reason of marriage, in the case of a woman, production of the marriage certificate will suffice as sufficient evidence. In other cases of change a deed poll or some other formal means should be produced.

3. Veterinary surgeons

The Veterinary Surgeons and Veterinary Practitioner's Registration Regulations 1967, made under the Veterinary Surgeons Act 1966, provide that the Register of Veterinary Surgeons must include the practitioner's full names, and any change of name after registration.

In the case of a woman who, on marriage, assumes her husband's name, the Royal College will register the change on production of a copy marriage certificate. In other cases a statutory declaration or deed poll will suffice. Whatever means is chosen the document should show the person's former names and the new name. This is to prevent any deception.

4. Medical practitioners

The Medical Act 1969 s 3(2)(c) provides that the Registrar of the General Medical Council must keep a register containing the names, qualification, address and dates of registration of the persons registered in it and any other particulars as may be prescribed by regulations made by the General Medical Council.

Alterations to a practitioner's registered name are governed by the Medical Practitioners Registration (No 1) Regulations 1981. The relevant Regulations are:

"9. (1) Subject to the provisions of Regulation 10, when a fully or provisionally registered person applies to the Registrar to have an alteration made in his registered name, or notifies a change of address, or applies for the registration of an additional qualification, the Registrar shall, on being satisfied that it is correct to do so, alter the register in order to give effect to the application.

10. (1) A person who applies to have an alteration made in his or her registered name shall be required to satisfy the Registrar as to his or her identity. If the alteration results from marriage, the person shall produce her marriage certificate or other official evidence of her marriage. In other cases, unless the alteration is insignificant, the Registrar may require a statutory declaration or other evidence of identity. Any questionable cases arising under this Regulation may be referred to the Registration Committee for determination.

(2) On the insertion in the register of an alteration in the name of a person, the Registrar shall also retain in the register the name of the person as previously registered."

The originals of any documents required must be provided; photocopies are not acceptable. A practitioner must also include with the application to register the change of name examples of both the former and the new signatures.

5. Dentists

The Dentists Acts 1957 and 1973 govern the practice and profession of dentistry. The management of the profession is regulated by the dentists professional governing body, namely the General Dental Council, 37 Wimpole Street, London W1.

The General Dental Council must keep a register of the names, qualification, address and date of registration of the persons registered in it (Dentists Act 1957 s 16). The Registrar must insert any alteration in the name and address of any person so registered which comes to his knowledge (Dentists Act 1957 s 23). The register is admissible as evidence of all the matters in it on mere production (s 16(3)).

Application for an alteration in the register by reason of change of name must be made in writing to the registrar. Where the change of name is by reason of marriage by a woman, the production of a copy of the marriage certificate will suffice. In all other cases a prescribed statutory declaration witnessed by a solicitor must be executed.

6. Nurses and midwives

Nurses and midwives too must notify any change of their name to their governing body. The evidence of change required will be similar to that outlined above.

7. Accountants

The Institute of Chartered Accountants and the Chartered Association of Certified Accountants will require evidence of a change of name by production of a copy of the marriage certificate where the change is by reason of marriage, or a statutory declaration or deed poll in all other cases.

8. Chartered surveyors

The Royal Institution of Chartered Surveyors has promulgated guidelines governing the practice for recording a change of name, as follows:

(a) except in the case of marriage or divorce, a member wishing to record a change of name, and/or obtain a Diploma in a new name, should furnish evidence of having changed his name by deed poll;

(b) in the case of marriage or divorce, less formal notification would be acceptable;

(c) any costs involved in preparing a new Diploma must be borne by the member;

(d) the old Diploma must be returned to the Institution.

9. Architects

The standard procedure of the Architects Registration Council of the United Kingdom is that when a person completes an application to come onto the Register in the first place, he or she provides three security checks—his or her date of birth, place of birth, and signature. If at some subsequent date he or she notifies a change of name, then the applicant is required to reproduce the signature in the old name and indicate the place and date of birth, which are then checked with the original.

Chapter 7

Effects of changing a name

Once a person changes his name, provided it is not done for any fraudulent purpose, he may use it for all purposes.

1. Marriage banns

If he intends to marry, he may publish his banns in the assumed name; see *Dancer* v *Dancer* (1949) and s 8 of the Marriage Act 1949.

2. Legal proceedings

In any legal proceedings the party must sue and defend in his new name. If the name is changed during the course of proceedings the court and all other parties to the proceedings must be notified and in such a case the action will continue in the new name but with all the documents recording the former name of the person in parentheses. No order to this effect is required: Practice Direction *Change of Surname* (1965) provides:

> "Where a party to an action changes his or her surname during the currency of the proceedings, his or her new surname shall be substituted and the former surname mentioned in brackets in all future proceedings therein."

The above practice applies to the county court under the provisions of s 76 of the County Courts Act 1984 under which the practice and general principles in the High Court may be adopted and applied to proceedings in the county court.

Furthermore, under Rules of the Supreme Court Order 20 rule 5(2), the court may grant leave to amend the proceedings to correct the name of a party, notwithstanding that the effect of so doing will be to substitute a new party, if the court is satisfied that the mistake sought to be corrected was a genuine mistake and was not misleading or such as to cause any reasonable doubt as to the identity of the person intending to sue or, as the case may be, to be sued. County Court Rules Order 15 rules (1) and (2) make similar provisions in respect of proceedings in the county court.

In a contractual situation a change of name may have the effect of frustrating a contract on the ground of mistaken identity if the effect is of negativing consent. In the context of criminal law, if the change of name results in deception, a change of name may not provide a defence.

3. Driving licences

A change of name must be notified to the Driver and Vehicle Licensing Centre, Swansea SA99 1BN (Road Traffic Act 1988 s 99 and the Regulations thereunder).

4. Passports and Department of Social Security benefits

In the case of a change of name by marriage the copy marriage certificate should be produced to the Passport Office or Department of Social Security, as appropriate. In the event of a change of name by adoption or by any other order of the court a certified copy of the order should be produced. Where a change of name has been effected by any of the methods outlined in Chapters 5 and 6, the production of a copy of the deed poll, statutory declaration, notarial instrument, advertisement in the press, certificate of record from the College of Arms, or special Act of Parliament, should suffice. In the case of a change of name by reputation, a letter from a professionally qualified person such as a doctor, lawyer, minister of religion, MP or JP, who has known the applicant in both names, testifying that the change has been effected for all purposes, would be acceptable.

In the case of minors, in the absence of any objections made to the Passport Office, a passport will be issued to a child on the consent of either parent. In the case of a child whose parents have never been married to each other the consent of the mother only is relevant. Where the child's name has been changed, a passport in the new name will only be issued if accompanied by a deed poll, adoption order or other court order permitting the change.

5. Company directors and shareholders

In the case of companies, the Companies Act 1985 s 10 and Sch 1 require that before the incorporation of a company the particulars of the former and present names and surnames of the directors and the secretary must be sent to the Registrar of Companies. Any alteration in the name of these individuals must also be notified to the Registrar within fourteen days (ss 288 to 290 Companies Act 1985).

Shareholders should notify the secretary of the company of any change in their names. It will depend upon the particular secretary to specify the evidence which the company will require to effect the change on the register of shareholders.

Appendix

Forms

Contents

1. Particulars of birth

FORM 1

PARTICULARS OF BIRTH

Regulation 7(1)		Births and Deaths Registration Act 1953, ss.1(1) and 5.
NHS Number	BIRTH	Entry No.
Registration district		Administrative area
Sub-district		

CHILD		
1. Date and place of birth		
2. Name and surname		3. Sex

FATHER	
4. Name and surname	
5. Place of birth	
6. Occupation	

MOTHER	
7. Name and surname	
8. Place of birth	
9. (a) Maiden surname	(b) Surname at marriage if different from maiden name
10. Usual address (if different from place of child's birth)	

INFORMANT	
11. Name and surname (if not the mother or father)	12. Qualification
13. Usual address (if different from that in 10 above)	

14. I certify that the particulars entered above are true to the best of my knowledge and belief

.... Signature of informant

15. Date of registration	16. Signature of registrar

17. Name given after registration, and surname

61

2. Declaration/statement by mother for the registration/ re-registration of a birth

FORM 2

DECLARATION/STATEMENT BY MOTHER FOR THE REGISTRATION/RE-REGISTRATION OF A BIRTH

Regulations 8, 16,
17(3)(a)(ii) Births and Deaths Registration Act 1953, ss. 9(5), 10(b)(i) and 10A(1)(b)(i)

CHILD		
1. Date and place of birth		
2. Name and surname		3. Sex

FATHER	
4. Name and surname	
5. Place of birth	
6. Occupation	

MOTHER	
7. Name and surname	
8. Place of birth	
9. (a) Maiden surname	(b) Surname at marriage if different from maiden surname
10. Usual address (if different from place of child's birth)	

INFORMANT	
11. Name and surname (if not the mother or father)	12. Qualification
13. Usual address (if different from that in 10 above)	

For use where the child is illegitimate and the mother produces a statutory declaration of paternity made by the father.

I, ... DO SOLEMNLY DECLARE that I am the mother of the child the particulars of whose birth are specified above and that the person named in space 4 above is the father of the child; and I request that his name should be recorded as such in the register of births.

Signature .... Date ....

Signed and declared by the above-named declarant in the presence

of ....
Registrar of Births and Deaths/Superintendent Registrar

.... Sub-district .... District

3. Certificate that name was given in baptism

FORM 3

CERTIFICATE THAT NAME WAS GIVEN IN BAPTISM

Regulation 14(1)(a)   Births and Deaths Registration Act 1953, s.13(1)

I .... of ....

do hereby certify that [according to the register of Baptisms for ....

.... now in my custody]* the $\frac{male†}{female}$ child stated to have been born on the ....

day of .... to ....

and .... was on the ....

day of .... baptised by ....

in the name ....

Witness my hand this .... day of ....

Signature ....

†Officiating Minister/Person having custody of register.

* To be deleted where the certificate is given by the person who baptised the child.
† Strike out whichever does not apply.

4. Certificate that name was given otherwise than in baptism

FORM 4

CERTIFICATE THAT NAME WAS GIVEN OTHERWISE THAN IN BAPTISM

Regulation 14(1)(b)   Births and Deaths Registration Act 1953, s.13(1)

I .... of ....

being the .... of the $\frac{male*}{female}$ child born to ....

and .... on the .... day of

.... whose birth was registered in the register of births for the

sub-district of .... on the ....

day of .... do hereby certify that the said child not having been

given a name in baptism was within twelve months after the registration of $\frac{his*}{her}$ birth given the

name ....

Witness my hand this .... day of ....

* Strike out whichever does not apply.

5. Statement by parent for the re-registration of a birth

FORM 5

STATEMENT BY PARENT FOR THE RE-REGISTRATION OF A BIRTH

Regulation 17(3)(a)(i)   Births and Deaths Registration Act 1953, ss. 9(5), 10A(1)(a)

CHILD	
1. Date and place of birth	
2. Name and surname	3. Sex

FATHER
4. Name and surname
5. Place of birth
6. Occupation

MOTHER	
7. Name and surname	
8. Place of birth	
9. (a) Maiden surname	(b) Surname at marriage if different from maiden surname
10. Usual address (if different from place of child's birth)	

INFORMANT	
11. Name and surname (if not the mother or father)	12. Qualification
13. Usual address (if different from that in 10 above)	

For use (a) where the informants give information out of the sub-district of the child's birth or (b) in any case where more than 3 months have elapsed since the date of birth of the child.

We .... being qualified under the Births and Deaths Registration Act 1953 to give information for the registration of the birth of the above-named child, DO SOLEMNLY DECLARE that the particulars above are those which are required to be registered concerning such birth, according to the best of our knowledge and belief, and request that the name of the father of the child be entered in the register of births as in space 4 above.

Signatures .... Date ....

Signed and declared by the above-named declarants in the presence

of ....
Registrar of Births and Deaths/Superintendent Registrar

.... Sub-district .... District

6. Statement by mother for the re-registration of a birth

FORM 6

STATEMENT BY MOTHER FOR THE RE-REGISTRATION OF A BIRTH

Regulation 17(3)(a)(iii)　　　　　Births and Deaths Registration Act 1953, ss. 9(5), 10A(1)(c)

CHILD	
1. Date and place of birth	

2. Name and surname	3. Sex

FATHER	
4. Name and surname	

5. Place of birth

6. Occupation

MOTHER	
7. Name and surname	

8. Place of birth

9. (a) Maiden surname	(b) Surname at marriage if different from maiden surname

10. Usual address
(if different from
place of child's birth)

INFORMANT	
11. Name and surname (if not the mother or father)	12. Qualification

13. Usual address (if different from that in 10 above)

For use where the child is illegitimate and the mother produces a certified copy of an order made under section 4 of the Affiliation Proceedings Act 1957

I, ... DO SOLEMNLY DECLARE that I am the mother of the child the particulars of whose birth are specified above and that the person named in space 4 above is the father of the child and is named as such in the certified copy of the order made under section 4 of the Affiliation Proceedings Act 1957 relating to the child and produced by me; and I request that his name should be recorded as such in the register of births.

Signature .... Date ....

Signed and declared by the above-named declarant in the presence

of ....
Registrar of Births and Deaths/Superintendent Registrar

.... Sub-district .... District

7. Deed of change of name (for enrolment)

This form can be adapted for change of forenames.

THIS CHANGE OF NAME DEED intended to be enrolled at the Central Office, Royal Courts of Justice, Strand, London WC2A 2LL made this .... day of .... One thousand nine hundred and .... by me the undersigned JAMES WORTHY [bachelor] [spinster] [single] [married] [divorced] [woman] [widow] [widower] of .... (*state address*) now or formerly called or known as JAMES RAGBONE
[a British citizen by birth] or
[a British Dependent Territories citizen as defined by section .... of the British Nationality Act 1981] or
[a British Overseas Citizen as defined by section .... of the British Nationality Act 1981] or
[a Commonwealth citizen as defined by section 37(1) of the British Nationality Act 1981]

WITNESSES and IT IS HEREBY DECLARED as follows:–

1. I absolutely and entirely renounce relinquish and abandon the use of my former surname of RAGBONE ("former surname") and assume adopt and determine to take and use from the date hereof the surname of WORTHY ("new surname") in substitution for my former surname of RAGBONE.
2. I shall at all times hereafter in all records deeds documents and other writings and in all actions and proceedings as well as in all dealings and transactions and on all occasions whatsoever use and subscribe the new surname.
3. I authorize and require all persons at all times to identify describe and address me by my new surname.

IN WITNESS whereof I have hereunto subscribed my former surname of RAGBONE and my new and assumed surname of WORTHY and have affixed my seal on the aforesaid date.

SIGNEDSEALEDANDDELIVEREDby the above-named JAMES WORTHY formerlyknownasJAMESRAGBONEin the presence of:

66

Name ....

Address ....

Occupation ....

Name ....

Address ....

Occupation ....

8. Deed of change of name (not for enrolment)

THIS CHANGE OF NAME DEED made this .... day
of .... One thousand nine hundred and .... by me the
undersigned JAMES WORTHY [bachelor] [spinster] [single]
[married] [divorced] [woman] [widow] [widower]
of .... (*state address*) now or formerly called or
known as JAMES RAGBONE

WITNESSES and IT IS HEREBY DECLARED as follows:–

1. I absolutely and entirely renounce relinquish and abandon the
    use of my former surname of RAGBONE ("former
    surname") and assume adopt and determine to take and use
    from the date hereof the surname of WORTHY ("new
    surname") in substitution for my former surname of
    RAGBONE.
2. I shall at all times hereafter in all records deeds documents
    and other writings and in all actions and proceedings as well as
    in all dealings and transactions and on all occasions
    whatsoever use and subscribe the new surname in substitution
    for my former surname to the intent that I may hereafter be
    called known and identified by the new surname instead of my
    former surname.
3. I authorise and require all persons at all times to identify
    describe and address me by my new surname.

SIGNED SEALED AND DELIVERED by
the above-named JAMES WORTHY
formerly known as JAMES RAGBONE in
the presence of:

Name ....

Address ....

Occupation ....

Name ....

Address ....

Occupation ....

9. Deed of change of name made on behalf of a child (not for enrolment)

This form can be used to change a forename, surname or both, but in the case of a baptismal forename, see pages 46–47 and 63.

THIS CHANGE OF NAME DEED made this .... day of .... One thousand nine hundred and .... by [me] [us] the undersigned JACK JONES (*name of parent or parents*) of .... (*set out the address in full*) on behalf of [my] [our] [child] [son] [daughter] ANTHONY JONES now or formerly called ANTHONY SMELLIE.

WITNESSES and IT IS HEREBY DECLARED as follows:–

1. On behalf of my said [child] [son] [daughter] [I] [we] absolutely and entirely renounce relinquish and abandon the use of [his] [her] former [forename] [surname] [forename and surname] of SMELLIE ["former surname"] and assume adopt and determine to take and use from the date hereof the surname of JONES ("new surname") in substitution.
2. On behalf of my said [child] [son] [daughter] [I] [we] shall at all times hereafter in all records deeds documents and other writings and in all actions proceedings as well as in all dealings and transactions and on all occasions whatsoever use and subscribe the new [forename] [surname] [forename and surname] in substitution for [his] [her] former [forename] [surname] [forename and surname] so relinquished as aforesaid to the intent that [he] [she] may hereafter be known or identified by [his] [her] new [forename] [surname] [forename and surname] and not by [his] [her] former [forename] [surname] [forename and surname].
3. [I] [We] authorise and require all persons at all times to designate describe and address [my] [our] said [child] [son] [daughter] by the new [forename] [surname] [forename and surname].

SIGNED SEALED AND DELIVERED
by the said JACK JONES on behalf of [his]
[her] above-named [child] [son] [daughter]
in the presence of:

Name ....
Address ....
Occupation ....

Name ....
Address ....
Occupation ....

10. Deed of change of name made on behalf of a child (to be enrolled)

This form can be used to change a forename, surname or both, but in the case of a baptismal forename, see pages 46–47 and 63.

THIS CHANGE OF NAME DEED intended to be enrolled at the Central Office, Royal Courts of Justice, Strand, London WC2A 2LL made this .... day of .... One thousand nine hundred and .... by [me] [us] the undersigned .... (*name of parent or parents*) of .... (*set out the address in full*) [single] [married] [divorced] [woman] [widow] [widower] on behalf of [my] [our] [child] [son] [daughter] ANTHONY JONES now or formerly called ANTHONY SMELLIE of .... who is seven years of age and [is a British citizen by birth] or [is a British Dependent Territories citizen as defined by section .... of the British Nationality Act 1981] or
[is a British Overseas Citizen as defined by section .... of the British Nationality Act 1981] or
[is a Commonwealth citizen as defined by section 37(1) of the British Nationality Act 1981].

WITNESSES and IT IS HEREBY DECLARED as follows:–

1. On behalf of my said [child] [son] [daughter] .... (*insert full new name*) [I] [we] absolutely and entirely renounce and relinquish and abandon the use of [his] [her] former [forename] [surname] [forename and surname] of

SMELLIE ("former surname") and assume adopt and determine to take and use from the date hereof the surname of JONES ("new surname") in substitution.

2. On behalf of my said [child] [son] [daughter] [I] [we] shall at all times hereafter in all records deeds documents and other writings and in all actions proceedings as well as in all dealings and transactions and on all occasions whatsoever use and subscribe the new [forename] [surname] [forename and surname] in substitution for [his] [her] former [forename] [surname] [forename and surname] so relinquished as aforesaid to the intent that [he] [she] may hereafter be known or identified by [his] [her] new [forename] [surname] [forename and surname] and not by [his] [her] former [forename] [surname] [forename and surname].

3. [I] [We] authorise and require all persons at all times to designate describe and address [my] [our] said [child] [son] [daughter] by the new [forename] [surname] [forename and surname].

SIGNED SEALED AND DELIVERED by the said JACK JONES on behalf of [his] [her] above-named [child] [son] [daughter] in the presence of:

Name ....

Address ....

Occupation ....

Name ....

Address ....

Occupation ....

11. Statutory declaration in support of change of name deed

I, ... of .... do solemnly and sincerely declare as follows:–

1. I am a Commonwealth citizen and a householder resident in the United Kingdom at the aforesaid address.

2. I have known the applicant .... (*insert new name in full*) formerly known as .... (*insert former*

name in full) for a period in excess of ten years since about
....
3. There is now produced and shown to me marked "A" a
    Change of Name Deed executed by the applicant on the ....
    day of .... 19 .... I identify the applicant
    .... (*insert new name*) with the person named in
    the said Deed.
4. There is also produced and shown to me marked "B" the
    following documents of the applicant ....
    (*insert new name*) formerly known as .... (*insert
    former name in full*):–
    [(i)   a certified copy of [his] [her] birth certificate]
    [(ii)   a certificate of [his] [her] citizenship by [registration]
            [naturalisation]]
    [(iii) a certified copy of [his] [her] marriage certificate]
    [(iv)   the notice of intention sent to [his] [her] spouse and
            the consent of the spouse]
    [(v)   the affidavit in support of the applicant's application.]

    The said .... (*insert new name in full*) referred to
    in the said Deed and in the above-mentioned documents
    as .... (*insert former name in full*) is one and the
    same person.
5. I make this declaration from my personal knowledge of
    .... formerly known as ....
6. I make this solemn declaration conscientiously believing the
    same to be true and by virtue of the Statutory Declarations
    Act 1835.

Declared by the above-named ....

at ....

this .... day of .... 19 ......

Before me,
A Commissioner for Oaths/Solicitor

12. Statutory declaration in support of deed changing the name of a child

I, ... of .... do solemnly and sincerely
declare as follows:–

1. I am a Commonwealth citizen and a householder resident in
    the United Kingdom at the aforesaid address.

2. I have known .... formerly known as
.... a [minor] [child] for a period in excess of ten
years [since his birth on ....] [since ....
I have known the [minor's] [child's] [mother] [father] [mother
and father] for a period of .... years since about
....

3. There is now produced and shown to me marked "A" a
Change of Name Deed executed by the said child's [father]
[mother] .... on the .... day of ....
19 .... I identify the person .... with the
person named in the said Deed.

4. There are also produced and shown to me marked "B" the
following documents of the said .... formerly known
as .... :–
    [(i) a certified copy of the Certificate of Birth]
    [(ii) the certificate of citizenship by [registration]
      [naturalisation]]
    [(iii) his/her consent (*where the child is sixteen years of age
      or over*)]
    [(iv) the consent of his/her [mother] [father]]
    [(v) the affidavit in support of his/her [father] [mother]]
The said .... (*insert new name in full*) referred to
in the said Deed and in the above-mentioned documents
as .... (*insert former name in full*) is one and the
same person.

5. I make this said declaration from my personal knowledge of
.... formerly known as ....

6. I make this solemn declaration conscientiously believing the
same to be true and by virtue of the Statutory Declarations
Act 1835.

Declared by the above-named ....

at ....

this .... day of ....19 ......
Before me,
A Commissioner for Oaths/Solicitor

13. Consent of spouse to enrolment of change of name deed

I, <u>MARY RAGBONE</u> of ....
the wife of <u>JAMES RAGBONE</u> of .... make
oath and say as follows:–

1. JAMES RAGBONE has given me notice of his intention to apply for the enrolment of the Change of Name Deed a copy whereof is now produced and shown to me marked "A" whereby he has now assumed the name of JAMES WORTHY instead of JAMES RAGBONE.
2. I consent to the said change of name and to the enrolment of the said Deed at the Central Office, Royal Courts of Justice, Strand, London WC2A 2LL.

Sworn by the said MARY RAGBONE

at ....

on the ....

before me,
A Commissioner for Oaths/Solicitor

14. Consent of wife and mother where husband executes a family deed

I, ... of .... am the wife of
.... formerly .... and the mother of the children referred to in the change of name deed attached hereto. I hereby consent to the change of name as set out in the said deed in respect of myself and my children, and to the enrolment of the deed in the Central Office, Royal Courts of Justice, Strand, London WC2A 2LL.

Signed ....
in the presence of:

Name ....
Address ....
Occupation ....

Name ....
Address ....
Occupation ....

15. Consent of a child over sixteen to change of name by deed

I, ... of .... am seventeen years of age
having been born on the .... day of .... 19 ....
I have read and approved the contents of the change of name deed
dated .... witnessed and declared by my [father]
[mother] [parents]. I agree to the change of my name from
.... to .... and to the enrolment of the
said deed in the Central Office of the Royal Courts of Justice,
Strand, London WC2A 2LL.

Signed ....

formerly known as ....
In the presence of:

Name ....

Address ....

Occupation ....

Name ....

Address ....

Occupation ....

16. Affidavit by married woman seeking dispensation from requirement for husband's consent to a change of name by deed

I, ... formerly known as .... of
....................., married woman, make oath and say as follows:

1.   I was married to .... on the .... day of
     .... 19 .... at the Register Office in the
     District of .... in the County of ....
     (*as on marriage certificate*). My maiden name was
     .... I was then .... years old, having been
     born on the .... day of .... 19 ....
2.   There are no children of our marriage.
3.   On the 1st of January 1990 I changed my name by deed poll
     from .... to .... I now wish to
     enrol the change of name deed and am informed by

74

.... and verily believe that I require my husband's consent so to do.

4. I make this affidavit in support of my application to dispense with his consent.

5. I last lived with my husband at .... in 1950 when he left me. I have had no contact with him since then, nor have I been aware of his whereabouts.

6. There are no relatives or friends of my husband who are now known to me through whom I could trace him.

7. My husband was unemployed when we parted. He had no bank account or other account as far as I am aware.

8. To the best of knowledge and belief he was not a member of a trades union or other professional organisation through which I may be able to trace him.

9. On the .... day of .... 19 .... my solicitors wrote to the Department of Social Security Special Records Section in Newcastle-upon-Tyne to ascertain whether the Department was aware of his whereabouts. A copy of the letter received is now shown to me marked "A". They do not have an address for him.

10. I know of no other inquiry that I can make to trace my husband.

11. Since .... I have been cohabiting with .... and have assumed his name.

12. The said .... is a married man, living apart from his wife. He has three children all of whom are adults.

Sworn by the said

at ....

on the ....

Before me,
A Commission for Oaths/Solicitor

17. Affidavit that change of name of a child is for the benefit of the child

I, ... of .... make oath and say as follows:

1. I am the mother of .... and make this affidavit

in support of my application to change the child's name from
.... to ....

2. I was married to .... on the .... day of
.... 19 .... The said .... was
born on the .... day of .... 19 .... She is the
only child of our marriage.

3. On the .... day of .... 19 .... my husband
left me and on the .... day of .... 19 .... we
were divorced. There is now produced and shown to me
marked "A" a copy of the decree.

4. Thereafter my former husband went to Nicaragua and failed
to communicate with me. I have tried to trace him through
the Nicaraguan Embassy but to no avail.

5. In .... I went to live with .... who is
divorced. He has four children, namely, ...
.... aged .... He has custody of the four
children. We have lived together as one family, and are
regarded in the neighbourhood as such.

6. My daughter .... attends the same school as the
said four children.

7. By a change of name deed executed by me on the ....
day of .... 19 .... I have assumed the name of
.... I wish my daughter to assume the same
surname and have executed a deed on her behalf which I
wish to be enrolled in the Central Office.

8. All efforts to trace her father have proved unsuccessful. I
know of no other steps which I could take to trace him.

9. The said .... also wishes my daughter to assume
his surname.

10. In the premises I respectfully submit it would be in the
interest and benefit of my daughter to be known by the same
surname as myself and my cohabitee and his children whom
she regards as her father and siblings respectively.

11. At present she is registered at school in the name of
.... This has caused considerable curiosity
among the children and has resulted in my daughter being
subjected to teasing and unkindness from other children.
This has caused her extreme unhappiness and distress. There
is now produced and shown to me marked "B" a report from
the head teacher which is self-explanatory.

12. In the circumstances I respectfully ask that there be leave to
enrol the change of name deed.

Sworn by the said

at ....

on the ....

Before me, ...
A Commissioner for Oaths/Solicitor

18. Advertisement of change of name by deed for publication in the London Gazette

I hereby give notice that by a Deed Poll dated the ...... day of
.... 19 .... and enrolled at the Central Office,
Royal Courts of Justice, Strand, London WC2A 2LL, I
.... (*insert new name*) of .... [single]
[married] [divorced] [a widow] [a widower] [a British citizen] [a
British Dependent Territories citizen] [a British Overseas Citizen]
[a Commonwealth citizen] renounced relinquished and abandoned
the name of .... and assumed the name of
....

Dated the .... day of .... 19 ....

19. Advertisement of change of name of a child by deed for publication in the London Gazette

I hereby give notice that by a Deed Poll dated the ...... day of
.... 19 .... and enrolled at the Central Office,
Royal Courts of Justice, Strand, London WC2A 2LL, I
.... of .... the [mother] [father] [mother
and father] of .... (*insert new name in full*) [an
unmarried child] and [a British citizen] [a British Dependent
Territories citizen] [a British Overseas Citizen] [a Commonwealth
citizen] renounced relinquished and abandoned the name of
.... and assumed the name of ....

Dated the .... day of .... 19 ....

20. Statutory declaration effecting change of name

I, <u>JAMES WORTHY</u> the deponent referred to in the Schedule hereto formerly known as <u>JAMES RAGBONE</u> being a British citizen by birth [or as the case may be] do solemnly and sincerely declare as follows:–

1. I absolutely and entirely renounce relinquish and abandon the use of my former name as specified in the Schedule hereto ("my former name") and assume adopt and determine to take and use from the date hereof the new name specified in the said Schedule ("my new name") in substitution for my former name.
2. I shall at all times hereafter in all records deeds documents and other writings and in all actions and proceedings as well as in all dealings and transactions and on all occasions whatsoever use and subscribe my new name in substitution for my former name so relinquished as aforesaid to the intent that I may hereafter be called known and identified by the new name and not by my former name.
3. I authorise and require all persons at all times to identify describe and address me by my new name.

I make this solemn declaration conscientiously believing the same to be true and pursuant to the provisions of the Statutory Declarations Act 1835.

THE SCHEDULE

Former name: JAMES RAGBONE
New name: JAMES WORTHY

Address:

Occupation:

Declared by the above-named Deponent
<u>JAMES WORTHY</u> formerly known as
<u>JAMES RAGBONE</u>

at ....

This .... day of .... 19 ......

Before me, ...
A Commissioner for Oaths/Solicitor

21. Statutory declaration effecting change of name of a child

[I] [We], ... the deponent referred to in the Schedule hereto the [mother] [father] [mother and father] of .... (*set out address*) do solemnly and sincerely declare as follows:–

1. On behalf of [my] [our] [child] [son] [daughter] .... now or formerly called .... [I] [we] absolutely and entirely renounce relinquish and abandon the use of [his] [her] former [forename] [surname] as specified in the Schedule hereto ("[his] [her] former [forename] [surname]") and assume adopt and determine to take and use from the date hereof the new [forename] [surname] specified in the said Schedule ("new [forename] [surname]") in substitution for [his] [her] former [forename] [surname].
2. On behalf of my said [child] [son] [daughter] I shall at all times hereafter in all records deeds documents and other writings and in all actions and proceedings as well as in all dealings and transactions and on all occasions whatsoever use and subscribe the new [forename] [surname] of .... in substitution for [his] [her] former [forename] [surname] of .... so relinquished as aforesaid and to the intent that [he] [she] may hereafter be called known and identified by [his] [her] new [forename] [surname] and not by [his] [her] former [forename] [surname].
3. On behalf of my said [child] [son] [daughter] I authorise and require all persons at all times to identify describe and address [him] [her] by [his] [her] new [forename] [surname].

I make this solemn declaration conscientiously believing the same to be true and pursuant to the provisions of the Statutory Declarations Act 1835.

THE SCHEDULE

Former [forename] [surname]:
New [forename] [surname]:
Address:
Occupation:

Declared by the above-named Deponent[s]

.... on behalf of [his] [her] [their]

[child] [son] [daughter] .... (*new name*)

at ....

This .... day of ....19 ......

Before me,
A Commissioner for Oaths/Solicitor

Index